Dating Playbook

Proven Tips, Lines, and Tricks to Pick Up Girls and Boys

(Dating Tips on How to Capture a Girl's Heart, Make Her Fall in Love With You)

Natalie Summers

Published By **Bengion Cosalas**

Natalie Summers

All Rights Reserved

Dating Playbook: Proven Tips, Lines, and Tricks to Pick Up Girls and Boys (Dating Tips on How to Capture a Girl's Heart, Make Her Fall in Love With You)

ISBN 978-1-77485-936-0

No part of this guidebook shall be reproduced in any form without permission in writing from the publisher except in the case of brief quotations embodied in critical articles or reviews.

Legal & Disclaimer

The information contained in this ebook is not designed to replace or take the place of any form of medicine or professional medical advice. The information in this ebook has been provided for educational & entertainment purposes only.

The information contained in this book has been compiled from sources deemed reliable, and it is accurate to the best of the Author's knowledge; however, the Author cannot guarantee its accuracy and validity and cannot be held liable for any errors or omissions. Changes are periodically made to this book. You must consult your doctor or get professional medical advice before using any of the suggested remedies, techniques, or information in this book.

Upon using the information contained in this book, you agree to hold harmless the Author from and against any damages, costs, and expenses, including any legal fees potentially resulting from the application of any of the information provided by this guide. This disclaimer applies to any damages or injury caused by the use and application, whether directly or indirectly, of any advice or information presented, whether for breach of contract, tort, negligence, personal injury, criminal intent, or under any other cause of action.

You agree to accept all risks of using the information presented inside this book. You need to consult a professional medical practitioner in order to ensure you are both able and healthy enough to participate in this program.

Table of Contents

Introduction 1

Chapter 1: The New Rules Of Attraction .. 3

Chapter 2: Let Dating Apps And Sites Work For You Instead Of The Other Way Around 16

Chapter 3: Why Most Guys Fail 27

Chapter 4: Now That I Have Your Attention... 31

Chapter 5: You Don't Need To Plan Dates 36

Chapter 6: Should Asking Women Out Be So Intimidating 42

Chapter 7: Sparks Ignite 53

Chapter 8: Respect Is Not An Exception . 62

Chapter 9: Dating Mistakes To Avoid 72

Chapter 10: Never Take Anything Personal 80

Chapter 11: The Nature Of The Dating World And The Current State 91

Chapter 12: Your Texting Game 95

Chapter 13: Dealing With Rejection 100

Chapter 14: Making Ageless Love Last . 107

Chapter 15: Ace The First Date 126

Chapter 16: Remain The Man Of Her Dreams 143

Chapter 17: How To Overcome Online Dating Hurdles 152

Chapter 18: Be Vulnerable And Stop Taking Things Too Personally 160

Chapter 19: How Do You Identify And Choose The Best Places? 167

Chapter 20: How You Perfect The Dialogue: Topics, Tips And Tricks 173

Conclusion 183

Introduction

Many people have heard this from their friends and colleagues. Women are often "complicated" and difficult to understand. It's because men don't care enough about the relationship to do so.

Attracting a lady is a slow process. You have to practice the moves before you go on the dancefloor.

There are many self-help and guidebooks that have been written on this topic. However, most men don't know what to do when they want to make a connection with someone. While I agree with the advice in those books, I feel men should have a more practical approach. They can apply it immediately to their lives, before and after they go out on dates, and then see the results.

That is what I tried to do with this book. This book was written to help you find answers to all of your burning questions. To help you discover your inner self and make the most of it.

Chapter 1: The new rules of attraction

"The meeting of two persons is like the contact between two chemical substances: if one reacts, both are transformed."

-Carl Jung

Although scientists understand the basics of physical attraction, it is still a complex concept. But, research and experiments have led to several theories on what attracts one person to the other. The decades-old psychological research that has shown that men find attractive qualities in women can be a great help to those who are searching for a partner or just looking for a date.

It's easier than ever to find dates online. It is as easy as filling out a comment box online or simply swiping left and right. How do men make lasting impressions on women in their 40s and 30s that will encourage them to click on their profiles and accept their date request? Women know that online profiles may not tell the whole story. Meeting up with someone online can lead to unexpected discoveries. It is not what men want to make a bad first impression on women. It is important for men to look attractive and surpass women's expectations.

Women are very selective about who they choose to date and for what reasons. It seems that women prefer men who have maturity. You don't want to appear ignorant about women's feelings and the rules of attraction on your first date.

While physical appearance can be a key factor in men's likeability and open up many doors for them, that doesn't mean you have to let your behavior slide. This chapter will focus on improving your appearance to attract the women you wish to date.

Attractive to Women

If you believe you'll receive a long list or recommended cosmetic products, you are wrong. There are compelling scientifically proven insights about traits and behaviors that can make you more successful. Surprisingly women are attracted to simple qualities found in men.

Be Kind

The halo phenomenon is one of psychology's greatest discoveries. What exactly is the "halo effect"? It is a bias that allows you to subconsciously allow one quality or trait to predict your character.

One example is the perception that beautiful people excel at their jobs.

Multiple studies support kindness' appeal. It doesn't have to be a big act of kindness. A simple gesture, such a as handing your girlfriend/wife a bouquet or listening, or even helping her carry her groceries, can improve your likeability and help increase her commitment to you. It is a sign of physical attraction. Research suggests that sex attraction can be boosted by genuine trustworthiness.

Additional studies have confirmed that people will perceive your body and face type as more attractive when you are honest and kind. Aside from the romantic benefits, kindness can also bring about a feeling of peace and tranquility. Research shows that people who give back to others are happier, healthier and have a longer lifetime.

Have fun with your partner

You and your partner will have a happier relationship if you share laughter together. Multiple studies have shown that women will be more drawn to men who can make their laugh than those who are good-looking. Surprisingly, men don't seem to be more attracted if women can make them laugh.

Laughing together can make a difference in your relationships. According to a University of Kansas research, those with a sense of humor or who share a similar sense of humor were happier in their relationships.

Researchers asked undergraduate students what they thought of their partner's ability make them laugh. According to the results, females valued both their partner's sense of humor as well their ability make their partner laugh.

Women appreciated men's ability to make them laugh. With all the life lessons you've learned, pick the most hilarious to bring out the humor in women.

Practice Mindfulness

Mindfulness has many benefits for improving the quality and quantity of your relationships. Dr. Marsha A. Lucas, author of Rewire Your Heart for Love, explains how mindfulness improves your relationships.

- Stress relief

When you feel stressed, it's more likely that you will react to minor problems. Trivialities can quickly get out of control, and before long you're having an argument with your partner, saying things you don't mean. Therefore, mindfulness meditation helps reduce stress levels and makes it less likely to lead to unnecessary arguments.

- Integrates Your Emotions and Intellect

Research shows that mindfulness practice can improve your connection between your intellect and your emotional brain. It allows you to manage your emotions more efficiently and effectively, which can help you win with women.

Empathy can be built

When you practice mindfulness, you will find that you are less focused on meaningless tasks and spend more time being conscious of your mind. This helps you to understand yourself and adapt to your feelings.

You will make your partner feel happier and more at ease if you're empathic. Empathy is about caring, kindness, empathy, and understanding. These things are the basis of any relationship.

Do Volunteer Work

Researchers from the UK showed 40 women photos of men. They also attached descriptions. About 30 women looked at photos of men and read brief descriptions about their hobbies.

This resulted in women rating men who volunteer more attractively than men who aren't. Because such men are compassionate and selfless, women find them attractive.

Be a leader

Some believe that leaders need to be able manage people. Leadership can be defined by the ability to guide and direct others through words and actions. Study after study shows that women desire to be with leaders, not dictators. It is important to provide feedback and set goals for the relationship.

- To prove that you are capable of leading, it is essential to think about the consequences of your decisions on your relationship.

- Selflessness is a sign that you care and are willing sacrifice your own needs to support your loved ones. Remember to keep your woman's needs in mind when you start a relationship.

- Start a relationship and show interest in activities which will benefit your relationship. It will solidify your connection with your woman by demonstrating your commitment to the well-being of your relationship.

Being emotionally available

Women can now buy their bread and clothing. Because today's women don't feel the need to have you come and show off your wealth, pretending that you are her savior, they do not require you to help them. She is fully capable of building her professional and personal life. All she asks for is your love, support and attention every step of this journey.

Let's pretend you have been on many dating dates. You were surprised to find out that you did not get a callback after some of the dates. Why? What went wrong This chapter covers everything you read.

Perhaps you were too focused on having a conversation about your emotional experiences, or talking a lot about yourself and your interests that you completely forgot about asking about her interests. This can make the woman question your commitment to the relationship.

If you talk all about yourself, even if a woman is interested, and you don't give her the chance to tell her about her experiences, or how she sees it, she won't be able to relate to you.

Therefore, you should put in effort and be emotionally available to your partner. Let the woman understand that she is valued and respected.

Recognize universal signals and look for them.

Helen E. Fisher is an anthropologist from Rutgers University. She says that women all over the globe show interest in the topic with a similar sequence.

She also shared this: Men should be aware that when a woman smiles back at her admirer and raises her eyebrows swiftly to look at him, before tilting her head down to the side and covering her face with her hands. This is when women expect men to be sexy and seductive, maybe offer a hook-up or continue flirting. Do not disappoint them by ignoring this gesture.

This pattern of flirting is so well-known, Irenaus Eibl Eibesfeldt an Austrian ethnologist was convinced that it is innate. The female flirting gesture was created eons back to signify sexual interest.

I don't want to talk friendship. Yes! You are correct. To have a successful relationship, you must connect on many levels with your partner.

This is where friendship shines. A National Bureau of Economic Research study shows that friendship can have positive effects on a relationship's well-being about twice when the partner is also their best friend. Friendship is crucial! It doesn't mean that your partner has to be your best friend. But friendship is crucial as it sets the stage for many other things. You might find that it is easier to establish a connection with her than you think.

Comfortable doing these things could indicate your commitment to the relationship. It also shows that you are enthusiastic to be with the woman in a serious relationship. It will show that you are putting in the effort to be there for her.

This chapter's moral is quite simple. As a man who has grown up, it's important to treat women as mature men. You should present these qualities to a woman when you meet her. She will be able to see the caring, friendly, and affectionate side of you and become attracted to you. After you have her interested, you can begin to flirt with your lady.

Chapter 2: Let dating apps and sites work for you instead of the other way around

Online dating sites have an interesting feature: they are designed to work for people who created them. It doesn't really matter whether you use an online dating site for free or a paid one. They all have the same goal: to maximize your chance of returning again and again. You can still make money from a site even though it is completely free.

Dating sites often have monetization features. Don't be fooled by their seemingly clean appearance. Paying dating sites are a great way to make money. If you choose to renew month-after-month, you are contributing dollars to the site's owners. This is the essence of dating sites, and it's something that you must remember.

These websites and apps for mobile dating have their own agenda. They may not work for you by default. It's a good thing to know all of this. It's obvious that these dating websites are not meant to allow you to quickly find your man. This means that you can adopt a strategy which will enable you to find the man you are looking for faster than others.

It's all just a numbers game!

The old saying is "To hit the Moon, you have to aim at the Sun." To put it in a dating context, if you want to have 10 dates, you need to reach out and touch hundreds of men. It is important to understand how statistics work. This applies to everyone.

Men who successfully use dating sites realize that it's a numbers-based game and respond accordingly. Because the rules are different for women, many women find a false sense comfort. Because men tend to seek the most, many women succumb to the temptation of thinking, "Well, since they are coming after me, I just need relax and sit back."

However, you must also play the numbers on your side. There is no way to automatically assume that the majority of men are going to win just because they have more women than men on a common dating site.

The interesting thing about modern dating is that women who don't look all that attractive actually go out on more dates that women who appear to be conventionally attractive. What's the reason? It's because women who struggle to get noticed are more likely to use an online dating service. Let me help you understand this. It is a good idea to assume that the quality and quantity of men you will attract will go up if they are willing to put in more effort.

You won't attract any men if all you do is be passive and wait for them to find you. Men will find you. However, it is not likely that you will attract guys you are interested in.

Percentages are the key to dating

As I said, dating is a numbers sport. It's all about the percentages.

To attract 100 guys, for example, to get one solid and high-quality guy. To attract 100 men, you need to be in front of thousands of men. Can you see how all this works? It's a filtration process. Remember how the percentage systems work.

Fact: Filtration is not always easy

You don't have to feel depressed. However, in order to attract 100 men, you profile must get in front thousands of men. That sounds pretty fair, doesn't it? Well, not quite.

The filtration can be quite brutal, as many of the thousands of males infiltrated are perverts. Looks are another topic. Can you imagine how frustrating this process can become?

It is sad to say that modern dating is filled with fake profiles. Many people mistakenly believe that all these fake profiles are for women. You are wrong.

Spammers have learned that flooding dating sites by creating fake profiles can earn a lot. They steal traffic from dating websites and redirect them to other sites. They are paid a commission every time someone they trick to sign up for an alternative webcam membership website or dating site.

Apart from spammers annoying people, fake men are common. These are men who claim to be single but have already been married. It is not uncommon for men to pretend to have millionaires even though they don't actually have any pennies.

The online presence of men trying to act like they are other men is alarming. It could be said that this is part and parcel of being a man. However, I don't think I have to give any details regarding the problems with perverts or jerks. I'm certain you can figure it out.

How to get your numbers game right

Knowing what you're up to, you should have a solid strategy for working the numbers. Otherwise you'll end up with less satisfying results. Even worse, you may attract the wrong guys if your not careful.

How do you leverage the numbers? The filtration process can be thought of as a giant funnel. The bigger the funnel, you have the better chance of having a steady stream of high-quality candidates who survive the filter. If your funnel is small, you might only get one guy to appear every few months. This is not the type of result you are looking for.

You are looking for candidates you can filter once you have agreed to meet on a first date. This is why you want to collect a sufficient number of potential dating candidates.

It is important to expand your reach before you can work with numbers. There are many areas in a large metropolitan area of the United States. One example is the San Francisco Bay Area, which has many distinct districts. There are three main areas in San Francisco: the East Bay,

South Bay, San Francisco and other parts. Make use of this advantage.

If you live in an area where it is easy to get to one side of town from the other, then consider including as many districts into your search parameters.

To work the numbers correctly, you must not rush. This is something that I cannot stress enough. If you're in hurry or act out desperation, it is possible to end up dating guys not in your target type range. These aren't the ideal men.

I'm not suggesting you should expect the perfect man. This is unlikely to happen. Let me just say that it might take some time for some guys to log in because they don't log in often. Many of them may have sent you messages or sent you messages, but it can take some time for them back in.

If you cut your list in a hurry or gave yourself a deadline, the candidates may not be chosen. It is crucial that you wait for these quality men to log in to your account so that you can make them available.

Last but not least, it is important to use templates when working in the numbers. It's not necessary to write a customized message for every inquiry. This is a total waste of your time. It is crucial to provide initial templates for those who first contact you.

Their first message is supposed to provide enough information for you to make a decision about whether or not to filter the messages. You should not expect a personalized response. It is much more efficient to have a template you can modify so you can quickly and efficiently filter the initial reply.

A quick introduction to hook up dating

Hookup dating is one of the hottest trends in America right currently. Hook up dating is quite different to traditional dating, as the ultimate goal isn't to have a boyfriend/partner. Hook up dating is just that, a quick hook up. It's all sex. It's all in the moment physical intimacy. In many cases, names don't even get exchanged.

It is important to ensure that you use the correct dating app or website. While many dating websites advertise themselves as traditional dating sites for men, they are often used by people as hookup sites. These websites are absolutely useless. This is particularly true when it concerns mobile dating apps.

Tinder and dating apps such as it are can be used for hooking up. However, it is vital to fully understand the usage of these websites or apps. It's possible to end up meeting people with very different expectations.

This is another reason to make sure you understand exactly what you are getting into. These are not areas for traditional dating. They aren't looking for potential partners. They are not looking to get married. They're just looking to have a good time. If this is what you want, get out of there fast.

Chapter 3: Why Most Guys Fail

Every woman fails to find the woman she wants. Unfortunately, many people fail. Many guys won't go out for the woman they love. They settle for someone they don't like because they are afraid of being rejected by more attractive women. There are many reasons they fail to attract the women they want. Most of these reasons depend heavily on the guy's image.

First and foremost, most men fail simply because they don't feel confident. As men, we do not naturally gain confidence. It takes work and dedication to be confident. Like a muscle, confidence can be described as an ability to build strength. You can train and strengthen it. Insecure men don't attract women. People dislike confident people. Humans love confidence, as it is a positive trait. Confidence makes a woman happy when she is with a confident man. Insecure men will not attract many women. This is because women don't want vulnerable men. Let me show you an example. Would you rather spend the night with someone confident and cool than someone anxious and fearful? Absolutely, we love to hang with confident people. In fact, your chances of being successful are greatly reduced if you lack confidence. Jane might choose to date George instead of John. They are both equally attractive. George is confident that he will ask Jane out, but John remains scared. Who do you think Jane might end up with?

The second is the neediness that many men possess. You might have had some conversations with women. Attractiveness is immediately destroyed when you are too dependent. If a man is constantly chasing down a woman 16x per day (even if they aren't married or engaged), the woman knows that he doesn't have any other responsibilities. You aren't worth your time if you're too dependent. It indicates that you are not busy. The woman is also aware of this. No one likes to be with someone who does not have a life and is boring. Consider the woman you are thinking about. Would you be willing to spend time alone with someone boring who doesn't have any interests? Hell no! I would prefer to date someone who is popular, successful, and has many hobbies. Never forget that attraction is killed by neediness

The third reason people are unable to date is due to their looks. I know that not everyone is the same. Everyone isn't Zac Efron. You will not get many women if your skin is really dark. There's a way out. You can improve your attractiveness by doing many things if you are naturally unattractive. You won't attract women if your body is less than 70% and you are at least 3 feet tall. Many pick-up artists say that looks don't matter. Looks do matter! It's true, I'm sorry. Women are not able to see visually more attractive men than very ugly ones, even though they may have the same skills, talents and mentality. There are many things you can do to improve your odds of getting ugly.

Chapter 4: Now That I Have your Attention...

My Chapter 3 advice will help you create a strong dating profile that draws attention. Your profile gets eyeballs. Men are responding to you profile. This is not the end. In fact, you are just at the beginning.

Attracting men is not the problem, I've said it before. Attracting only the right guys is. First, you must know how many men you are getting. Then you will need to filter this base.

Convert men you attract

It is vital to understand the difference between converting or attracting. A lot of men online play the numbers games in a very lazy way. If you think you are playing the numbers games, you should understand that many other men are doing the same thing. They will respond to almost anything that looks humanoid with a heartbeat. So don't surprise if you attract guys from your target group who might not be attracted or convert to dates.

Keep in mind that attraction is different from conversion. Conversion means that these people are more likely to get to know you personally. They are happy to go on a date. Attracting simply means someone clicked on an image and sent you messages. Anyone can do that. There is a big distinction between the two.

Continue to filter

It is important to filter any email they send you quickly. Use an email template to filter males based on your target type, as I mentioned earlier. You should be extremely harsh at this stage. Do not show compassion on anybody. If you give these guys an inch, they'll go the distance. They would not hesitate to use you and abuse your body.

It is important to filter guys off, even if they are off by a little. If the guy you are interested in is not even 1% like your target, don't feel obliged to reply. You can also set up rejection emails templates. These guys have gotten used to it. You don't want to be the Mother Theresa for online dating. These guys aren't going to need your sympathy.

Be sure to keep the right ones

After you have sent the initial filter email and received the feedback you want, you can move on to the next step. You are still filtering and don't have any time for settling. Do not get discouraged. You can't compromise by changing your standards. You have to get to the truth.

After they answer, ask them directly if you share their interests. This is vital. This is crucial, regardless of his looks. It is important to quickly filter the man. It's important to remind him about the shared interests that you are looking for. Don't be afraid of expressing your preferences. Also, don't worry about offending people's feelings.

This will be noticed by him. Guys who are really interested in what you are interested will continue to be interested. Guys who are caught playing games will be caught in a lie. Ask questions. Do not hesitate to ask questions. They will eventually fall for lies because it takes more to lie than to tell truth.

Keep on your toes. Click the delete key if there is any sort of inconsistency or discrepancy. It is better than to regret making a wrong decision about going out on a romantic date with someone unsavory or potentially dangerous.

Open books can get boring

Even though you are engaged in a backand forth with these men, it is important to remember that many women fail at this stage. They don't mind being open. They don't believe in mystery. They simply tell the guy all they know. Their lives are open to interpretation.

While it is important to be clear about what you are trying to do when engaging people in your life, you don't have to give away everything. The guy will keep coming back to you if there is some mystery. Many women give up at this point. Men end up dating women who are not very attractive but still know how to play the mystery.

Chapter 5: You Don't Need To Plan Dates

However, I want to be clear. This is not to say that you shouldn't have something planned. You should have a general idea of where and what activities are most important. You don't need to have a detailed plan. It doesn't make the date any more special. You don't need to have an elaborate plan. Keep it simple. Let's take a look at "the minimum plan."

The Minimal Plan

The minimum plan should not include reservations for dinner. It shouldn't be about buying movie tickets you need to arrive on time. Open communication and good vibes, are the two main ingredients of a great first date. Your minimum plan should be to go somewhere and do something you are comfortable with.

Here are some examples of how a minimal plan might look.

Enjoy lunch at a casual and relaxed place.

You both will find it beneficial to go to lunch somewhere casual. Fancy dinners can help you to begin a new relationship. You don't have to be impressive. You don't have to be the most impressive. You want to be easy going.

You can talk to your date by having a casual lunch. It lets you wear what you'd normally wear. It's not necessary to dress up, it's not necessary to be polite and you don't need to impress anyone. It doesn't matter if you are dressed up or not. You just need to be yourself.

Spend time outdoors.

If you love the outdoors, go to a beach, boardwalk or Pier, or any place you feel most comfortable. If you don't love the outdoors, don't go. You want to be comfortable. If your partner can't stand the one place you truly enjoy, it is possible to end the relationship before things get worse. You are not in a relationship to give up what you love. You are trying to date someone you enjoy the same things that you. If this means that you and your dog go to a dog beach, a dog park, or that you have sandwiches at a park with your dog, then do it.

It's possible to strike up a conversation outdoors without worrying about having to be surrounded by dozens of others. It allows you to be your true self without worrying about others. You can ask her all the questions that you want, and then answer any she asks. There is no better way to express yourself than when there is plenty of open space around.

Do something you would share with your friends.

You can make a list with all your friends of the things that you do together. Make a list of all the things you do with friends. Now think about what you could do with a potential girlfriend. You can choose what you are most passionate about and "make it a plan". But not one that is too complicated. Simple plans will make her feel that you actually have a plan.

It's easy to be normal when you go out on a date with girls. It will force you to behave differently than usual by planning a fancy dinner and going to a movie she would enjoy. You want to show your woman exactly who you are, so you can do what you've done before.

Why a woman meets her first man on a date

A woman is on a first date with you because she already loves you. Simply put.

You should think about it. This woman is not blindly going on a date without knowing anything. This woman has likely met you before. If she hasn't met you before, it is likely that she has heard a lot about your life or seen you in person. She has already decided she likes and wants to go out on a date. If she didn't already love you, she wouldn't go on the date.

This is why you don't have the need to impress a lady. I'm not suggesting you show her that you don't care. I am saying that you need to understand that just because she likes you, it doesn't mean you have to do anything. Simply be you and go where you want.

If a woman feels you should have worked harder to impress her first date, this is not the woman you want. You don't want to impress women who are more concerned about how much money they spend than how beautiful you look. It's the kind of woman who demands that you compliment her on how beautiful and attractive she is. You want a real woman. You want a woman who is open to you being yourself, and who also respects you.

Do what feels natural to your body

Do what you love. Do what interests you. Keep the first date relaxed and fun. You want to feel comfortable enough to let her know who you are. It is important to get to know the woman you are interested in without trying to force it to work. A relationship can't be forced to work. It will just work out. It is always best to be yourself at the beginning. If it works it is good. If it doesn't, it's a good thing that you didn't pretend to be someone else and fall into a trap of deception throughout the rest of your relationship.

You will notice that your first date went well and you'll know she was enjoying you.

Chapter 6: Should Asking Women Out Be So Intimidating

"Don't let fear stop you from striking out."

-Babe Ruth

It's not easy to ask women out. You are afraid of being rejected. Fear of being laughed at in her group chat where you share your failed attempt to ask her out with other girls. Or you might be embarrassed and remember the incident every day for five more years. Perhaps you thought she was being infatuated with you but she was actually polite.

Relax, if she flirts with you and shows any of the signs mentioned in the previous chapters, chances are that she is interested but waiting for you.

Today, women will often ask men out. However, if you were confident and assertive, this is something women want in a man. It will definitely increase your chances to get a yes. You may be thinking, "But, won't that make me seem needy and desperate?". If a woman likes to you - and as far as we can tell, this woman is into you - then she will not be making any such remarks or thinking about you in that way.

This is due to a deeply-rooted social script that states men should be the pursuers and women should be the ones pursuing them. While it's not written in stone Neeta Vi Shetty, a psychotherapist and life coach, believes this to be a result of women being shy and believing that the job is theirs.

You are the one who is responsible for everything. Make the first move. However, before you do so, make sure that you are fully prepared. Here are some guidelines to help get you started.

It is important to choose the right time

Let's say that you made the first step, but didn't have time to make it right. You don't want your attempt to ask her out to be like the "right person, wrong timing" scenario. To increase your chances of succeeding, you should look for the right time to ask her out when you are together.

Setting the mood

The best time to ask someone out is when they are having a great day. You have a great relationship with her. You can feel the chemistry between you and your romcom. At this point, you can strike. This will make it easier for her to accept your offer. Waiting for the right moment is not a good idea.

It does not need to be perfect. It does not have to be perfect.

You might be walking on campus or visiting a friend's house. You can approach her and start a conversation.

If you and your partner have been communicating on a dating site or any other form social media, and it is going well from both sides without any small talk, then try your luck. Ask her to come to a bar with your to enjoy a drink, or invite her to visit you at home. If you have a personal or funny story to share with her, this is the best time to ask her out. This establishes a private relationship.

Catching Her Off Guard

You must ensure that she is completely attentive before you ask a girl out. You may have caught her off guard by her distractions, such as a friend's death or disappointing test results. If this happens, you will most likely be refused. Make sure she's happy by laughing, watching a movie she loves, and discussing topics she likes.

Don't take her by surprise. It's not a good idea to ask her out just because. It'd be a good idea to flirt with her occasionally in an unsubtle way, such as by "accidentally", touching her or making eye contact.

It is best not to ask her out in front her friends. It might scare her away completely. Friends can be very nosey and well-meaning. This can cause anxiety or shyness.

Be a Gentleman

Asking a girl out on a date is difficult. It's not easy to ask a woman out on a date. It's possible, but chances of you succeeding will drop to nearly zero. Women won't like men who disrespect boundaries and ignore social rules for proper dating. It's possible to come across rude and uncoordinated.

Be genuine

Pickup lines are not recommended. They are useless. Pickup lines never work. Women know this. There is no conviction in them. Therefore, women will notice that you don't care about her personally. You are simply trying to find random women and anyone who is willing to give you a yes. Be open with her. Tell her if she wears a particular outfit or if you love the fragrance. Women love honesty, and they can sense fake smells from afar.

Be Patient

The girl doesn't have to be in a hurry to say yes. It is okay to not press the girl for an answer. She should be allowed to take her time and think about it. It is not a good idea to speak too strongly. This will overwhelm her. It is best not to call or message her so much that it becomes annoying. Don't forget that people live their lives and don't necessarily owe any time to you. Avoid being dependent and clingy. It is an unattractive characteristic that can negatively impact your relationships with girls.

Learn how to take a no

It won't mean the end of your world if the girl doesn't like you. There will always be others and eventually, one will say yes. Do not lose hope and don't allow rejections to define your self-worth. If she doesn't say yes, you can be kind to her. Some men react badly when they are turned down and project that emotion onto the girl. It can get ugly. You won't get a second chance even if it was just a sliver of a chance.

The "Don'ts" when asking a woman out

Don't be insensitive

Don't try to make yourself appear tough. Most women can see past the mask and don't appreciate the tough guy act. Be authentic and you are who you are. Being emotional does not make you less of an individual. Studies show that women love men who are interested in cats and babies. Show her how you care for her.

Do not let your guard down

Simply nodding your head at a girl's story is not enough. This is rude and off-putting and shows that you don't listen to what she tells you. Make sure to listen to her and show interest if you want to be friends with the girl. Ask the girl questions about her story. Bonus points if it is something you can remember in the future or use as a reference for something else. You can be kind and compassionate with her when she confides that she is having an awful day.

Talking is a good thing.

The silent brooding persona doesn't work in real life. A woman wouldn't want to go out with an automated robot. Let the girl know your worries and fears. It shows that you have a personality.

Don't Be Negative

Talking about worries is one thing. It is another when you complain about everything and act negatively. You don't have to act like a whiny boy when you're on a first date with a girl. It will repel the girls, and you'll be back on your first date.

Be realistic and don't hold on to too much hope

You are not out on a "date with your crush just because she has decided to go out for coffee or dinner. It can be an indication that she values you as a friend, and would enjoy spending more time with you, but not just platonically. This can also signify that she's trying to get the best of someone else. You already know that she is into you and you will be able to stop her from going on more dates. Don't expect too much and you will regret it. Keep it light and have a conversation with your partner if things become serious.

Don't Be Superficial

Looks are important but they shouldn't be the only thing about the girl that you want to go out. It is fine to compliment her on how beautiful she looks. But, if all you focus on is her looks, it will get tedious quickly. Tell her what you like about her. She might be funny or incredibly talented. Give compliments. It will make her feel happy and put a smile in her eyes. After a while, she may stop being interested in you telling her how pretty her face looks or how hot it is.

These rules are a great way to win a girl's heart. If you play your cards correctly and pay attention to what you say, you can make sure they love you. Confidence is the key to success, no matter how clichéd it may sound. Even if your feelings are the exact opposite, perform a performance until you get it. Don't be afraid to be vulnerable with yourself. You don't have to appear different in order to impress others. You won't be able to win the long-term, and you'll lose your identity. If she loves you, it will be because of who you are. This will ensure that you have a healthy, happy relationship. You can only control your fear. It is possible to conquer your fears and have the whole world in your grasp.

Chapter 7: Sparks ignite

Tired of being the sole one in the circle? Are you fed up of being the third person on your friend's dates? Are you too pretty to be alone for dinner dates? After the breakup with your lover, have you been moping about in your living room? Are you sick of hating the idea and feeling hopeless about love? Now is the time to look into dating. Get up, get dressed and ready to go into the dating world.

Before you go on the rollercoaster ride known as dating, there's one thing you need to be aware of and reflect upon. Yes, finding your soulmate is great. You can share with this person all your struggles and joys, and you'll create a bond that will bring you together happiness unlike any other. Don't let your happiness be dependent on one person. If you go into a relationship with such a mindset, you might cause more damage than is necessary. Don't be afraid to be positive. But, don't forget that you must always give something back to yourself. This will keep you happy no matter the outcome.

To be successful in this field, you need to get into the right mindset for dating. But being single for too many years might have put you off your game. NBSBs (No boyfriend/girlfriend since birth) and NGSBs(No girlfriend/boyfriend since birth) have a harder time trying to date. The biggest problem people have is not knowing where to start. What is the first, second, and third thing I should do? What are the important things I need? These are my goals. How do I get them accomplished? Where do I find 'the One'? How do you know if this is the right man or girl to be with? You might even have second thoughts about someone you are considering dating, or if they are your current partner. Before you go out on a date, there are many things to keep in mind.

These are 8 easy tips to simplify the complicated world of dating.

1. Make sure you have high standards. You won't settle with less than what you are worth. This is the first step you must take before you can even consider dating. This may make you wonder why it is so important. This is the simple answer. Logically speaking standards will narrow down your chances to meet your future

lover. It is difficult to find the right person for you if you don't know what you are looking for. It is important to be clear about what standards are. There are too many standard because it is like having a mental check-list. If you have too much to check, your chances of finding the perfect match to your standards will be reduced. Because dating is about compatibility, it's important that you are interested in your standards. It is important to find two people who share your common interests and needs in order to build a relationship. If there is too much disagreement early in a relationship, it will lead to problems for both of you.

2. Don't be afraid of setting priorities for yourself. Remember the first point I made about dating? It is not a good idea to put all your sunshine in one pot. If you lose it, nothing will remain. However, this does not mean that you should limit your time

and give it all up to someone you love. This does not mean that you should give up your time or attention to your date. That would be extremely rude. That is why I say that you can go to the fitness center 3 times per week if it suits your schedule. Do not feel constrained by your time due to the fact that you have met someone. If you really like the person, they will adapt to your schedule. You must give your date the time and attention it deserves in order to move on to the next level.

3. You must also know when you need to move on. Some dates may not last forever. Some couples go on for 2 to 3 more times. Don't be afraid of giving up if it isn't working. Do not waste your time on things that are not going according to plan. There is a good chance that one person feels the same way as the other. Not being on dates with someone does not make you a committed partner for life. If it doesn't

work out, you shouldn't feel guilty about ending your relationship with that person. Tell the truth to yourself and to your date. You can't lie about the simple things. This isn't the way to successful relationships and dates. If you lie to yourself about your date, it will make it difficult for you to leave the relationship and be open to new possibilities.

4. Every date is a chance to feel the same way. This is how I want you to feel after every date. It is vital that you get the right attention from your date. It is the kind that makes you feel happy about both of your activities. It must feel natural, good and easy. You should feel that your date respects you as an individual. You don't have to feel any unpleasantness from your date. That is because they are giving you the wrong kind attention. If you feel disregarded, worst, molested or abused at any time, don't hesitate to leave the

relationship. You don't need this kind of vibe around your life. It will only make you feel worse. Tip #3 should be followed and then you can move on. You don't need to waste more time with assholes or bitches who take you for granted but treat you better than you deserve.

5. The key to successful relationships is patience. It might seem that you are too young to consider long-term relationships. Stable dating will lead to this, so you might as well be the right mindset. Unless you are someone who is just looking to play around. Which I doubt you are, because you are reading my words. However, I want you to know that you can't expect to have a serious relationship with someone one day. Don't be afraid to take some time for yourself and your date to connect and breathe. Trust me, it will get you to where you are both looking for. Relax and let go of all thoughts about what the next steps

are. The fun of your relationship is ruined if you become too involved in every little detail. Enjoy the moment and enjoy it.

6. The most important thing is to remain brave. All of the above tips require you to be brave. You must be brave enough for you to speak up for yourself, and for the things that matter to you. It takes courage to say no, even when it doesn't work out. You should also have the courage to believe you are doing right.

The only thing that can stop you from falling in love with someone is you. You can only fall in love when your heart and mind believe it should. It is not easy to get to this moment if one starts at the bottom. I can't give you a list of your standards. I can't help you decide when it is best to prioritize. I cannot tell what to do with your time. I can't know what your feelings are. I cannot show you how patience works. I can't make you brave. All these decisions are up to you. But I can assure you that once you find love, you will do it with and for the "right one".

Chapter 8: Respect is not an exception

While you'd hope this wouldn't be necessary to be stressed, if there is one thing I've learned from coaching... it's the fact that common sense isn't really all that common.

Even through the most difficult arguments, keep your communications respectful and kosher. You must create an environment that allows you two to communicate freely.

Be aware of your humor, whether it is sarcasm and flippant. These things can endanger your woman over time and make her question your motives. It might seem unlikely that this would occur, but women are more sensitive than you think. This is no stretch, especially if you are taking a stance on their egos and the things they love or pride themselves in. Let go of the humor and try to focus on the things that are important.

Keep your communication professional. It will show her that you don't appreciate her and she'll lash back at you.

It sets the tone and will make any argument that follows a disagreement a bitter one. It's not friendly, often counterproductive, an indicator of relationships that are not lasting or even work.

Don't ridicule her or make it a point to make fun of them. You don't have to agree with her, even though she can be self-deprecating if she chooses. Aren't men sometimes self-deprecating in order to get validation and to settle their insecurities. Be respectful of her when she is with her friends. This will set you up for an emotional confrontation in which you make her feel like she is 2 inches tall, very emasculated, embarrassed. You should think about why she would make such remarks.

Be kind and respectful to your woman. But, remember that mutual respect is earned, but can be chipped away faster than you might think.

You don't need to be extraneous in your compliments.

Men's dating advice columns tend to recommend complimenting women.

It is not clear if it is something she is unique in, something physical or her intellect. But the theory is omnipresent. If you compliment her, she will immediately warm up to your compliments.

It is not a mistake, but we rarely actually take action on this front.

Men don't like complimenting other men, even close friends. We live in a world where we don't receive a lot of positive reinforcement. Men get most compliments on work. That's nice. But it doesn't provide the self-esteem or selfworth-boosting comments that can really improve someone's mood.

You can't picture a group of men getting together and complimenting one another's boots or shirts.

This is a point that needs to be repeated: male-male interactions don't tend to be complimentary or positive vocally. So they don't receive many compliments each week. This is normal for us. But, for our women, it should be more!

Be kind to your woman by complimenting her and letting her know that she is appreciated for what she does. Men should pick the most flattering shirt for their woman. She is smart and can fix anything for you. Gush about how wonderful she looks for date nights, and how talented and dedicated she is to her hobbies and work.

Some of this may feel fake and unnecessary. You don't need tell her how it feels for her to feel that you appreciate and respect her.

However, think about all the reasons women want to get an engagement ring. Sometimes women need more than knowing someone cares about them. Proclaim it loudly. It unites you.

Better still, compliment her when she's insecure or uncertain about something. It's great if you can compliment her on those things. She will feel more confident and self-confident.

It is important to make her feel appreciated. She will be more inclined to do the same for yours, it is guaranteed.

What is your actual face saying?

Sometimes, emotions are sent that we didn't intend or we just give too much of ourselves away. It doesn't matter what situation you're in, the key is to align your appearance with your emotional state. This will ensure that you aren't transmitting mixed messages, and worse, causing misunderstandings.

It's crucial to learn how you can pass the mirror test.

What is the mirror testing? It's about feeling an emotion and seeing how your body and facial expressions communicate that emotion. Do they align? Do they show emotion? Do you get mixed messages from people?

For example, smile and laugh when someone gets angry or nervous.

How does your woman respond to your angry gaze, smile, frowning, crossed arms and cross-eyed stare?

This is something that you must figure out and maintain. Any misalignment in the external and inner representations of an emotion can result in a misunderstanding between you and your woman. Your ability to accurately represent how you feel inside is essential. It keeps things simple and honest, as well as avoiding any kind of reading between lines by your lady. Women can often draw incorrect conclusions and read too many lines, as we all know.

Smile when you're happy. It seems so easy, doesn't?

Our subconscious often takes control of our ability to withdraw and protect us. Do not assume that your body language during a heated conversation or argument is open-minded, accepting, and friendly. You were actually standing with your arms folded and your voice raised?

The mirror test, although not always apparent, can help set the tone for a relationship without any hidden messages or underlying anger.

She is not to be criticized, but the consequences.

It is likely that you receive or give criticism on a daily base. You may have to give or receive criticism as part of your job, or it could be an integral part. It isn't ideal but it's a reality. In the context of a relationship however, criticism should not be used lightly, but with care.

There are many reasons for criticizing someone in your day. Working with someone can help you improve your performance. On public transport, you might be complaining about someone's odor. To your friends, it could even be a residual of other resentments.

Critique must be used to enhance your relationship with your lady.

It is important to remove any emotion that criticism may bring. Instead, focus on the things you wish to achieve from criticism. You are simply trying to bring things to her attention, to work them out, and hopefully to fix them or teach you how to better deal with them.

It's best to be logical and avoid strong emotions.

None of them can resolve the underlying cause that has so disturbed you.

Don't criticize her for the actions. Instead, focus on how they make you feel. It's far better to be able to rationally talk about your emotions, and then re-align yourself with the consequences that you share with them.

Instead of focusing on making it worse, choose your words carefully. You might be denying her something very important, which could only lead to more resentment. But, if your words are direct and you address the emotional consequences, she may decide to change. This is far better than complaining.

Chapter 9: Dating Mistakes To Avoid

Men can do stupid things, especially if there is a woman who they like. It can make them do some really stupid things when they're trying to court women. This could lead to a disastrous relationship. Here are some dating mistakes to avoid.

No Game Plan

Without a plan in place, it is impossible to show up. While I'm not saying you should have a plan in place, it helps to have a framework. While you cannot be strict about everything in your life, you need to have an idea of where you want it to go. A plan must be created that outlines what you want to do and where you will go for the date. It should also outline what your options are. It shows you are organized and have the ability to make decisions. A pushover is not something that anyone likes. How can you avoid becoming a pushover? Consider this question before you decide to meet up with your date. What will we do afterward? What will we do?

Not being a good listening person

Sometimes men forget to listen to what their girlfriend says or ignore what she has to say. It can be frustrating when someone repeatedly asks the same question. You will feel the same about your date if she doesn't pay enough attention. Remember that the purpose of the date should be to get to understand her better. This cannot happen if you don't pay attention to what she has to say. You should not be too self-absorbed to hear what she has to offer. Be sure to remember everything she's said about her likes. It is not uncommon for women to drop subtle hints so be ready to listen. To ensure you are attentive and able to listen, pay close attention to her words and keep a few key points in your mind. This will show that you are listening and you can either quote her or refer to them while talking.

Don't make contradictory assertions

This one's for men who have a tendency to say, "I don't want a serious partnership," and then quickly feel emotions. Do not say, "maybe it is better to be friends" before going into bed. Do not be afraid to tell her what you want. You may be seeking the same things she is looking for, and keep telling her that this is not what you want. Being truthful is the best policy so that you don't get caught saying something contradictory.

Don't be a Bad Wingman

This is for the men who bring their friends to "entertain," their date's friend as he tries to make it with his chosen target. Be a good wingman by bringing someone along. If he can't have a meaningful conversation with his friend, how will you ever get along with him? Flying solo is the best way to go, even if you have a friend. Just make sure he knows what he's doing.

A lack of confidence

The lack of confidence is the worst thing that can happen. Confidence can be your most attractive accessory. If you lack it, it will ruin your date. But be careful. There's a fine line between appearing confident and being arrogant or too confident. You don't want to come across pompous. While you may appear confident, your façade will eventually fall apart. Your self-confidence is the best thing you can do. Your confidence shows in how you speak, your posture, and your body language.

Not being Gentleman

It doesn't necessarily have to be offered to pay for the date. However, it is considered chivalrous to pay. It is the same with holding doors. While she may be able to open the door herself, if you hold it open for her it will show that you are generous and kind. You'll leave a lasting impression on her by the kind gestures that you show. So how can you make sure that you don't seem like a man? Assist her by holding the doors open, making sure she is seated before taking the seat. Offer to pay for her dinner and treat her like a lady.

Being Mean

Many movies portray women as being brash and rude. They get paid to do their parts! If you come across to her as rude, she will probably never let you go out again with you. Although being a little bit snarky can work well for some, it is a line you must not cross. Nobody likes being treated unfairly by others. Be kind even when you laugh.

Expecting to have sex

Yes, you will find times when your sanity is compromised. It's OK if this happens. However, this does not mean that you should expect sex at any point in the relationship. It's not possible to build solid relationships with people when you stop using dates as a means of getting some action. Never expect to get sex on the first date. Expect to be rewarded if things go your way.

Don't use poor pickup lines

A good pickup can make a great icebreaker. However, a poor one can turn into a deal breaker. Stop saying things such as "Excuse moi, I dropped something!" Your jaw is clenching!" Use corny, cheesy, or even worse pickup lines. You should not be using poor pickup lines. Use genuine compliments instead. Even if your compliment doesn't go through, you will still look intelligent for not using a bad pickup-line.

Texting inappropriate

Texting is a common error that many men make. There is a place and time for each text that you wish to send. If someone informs you of a family member's death, it may not be a good idea if you tell them that in the next text. No inappropriate or explicit messages, jokes or images should be sent, even if they have sexual undertones. You could be hurting your chances of getting any real progress. Before you ever text someone, consider whether it is something that you are comfortable with others asking. Before you send anything to her, find out what her emotions are and how comfortable she is.

You can make it easier to find the woman you want by avoiding these mistakes. You can avoid these potential pitfalls by having a little common sense and being present.

Chapter 10: Never Take Anything Personal

This is a section I feel we should include before we begin our journey. Do not take anything personal! Some women can be extremely cruel and mean. I recommend that you change your mindset. You must believe in yourself as the MAN. You must walk, talk, feel confident. It is not necessary to be proud, but self-assured. Believe in yourself and believe you can give your daughter the best physical, emotional, and mental experience. It will show through the way that you speak, walk, and act.

Your best self is possible if you work hard! Read self-improvement literature. If you don't have enough time, audiobooks are an option. If you don't have a gym membership, get one and begin working out at least 3 times per week. You will be amazed at the positive effects it has on your brain. Google "workout regimen" if it isn't already. And, hey, you might even meet someone there. Win-Win, my friend! To help you break out of your shell if you're introverted, you might consider taking acting classes and improv classes. I found it helped me, being an introvert.

The "Meetup application" is free to download for IOS or Android. Meetup allows you to meet people in person by connecting with them based upon your mutual interests. Meetup helps people meet new people and learn new things. It also allows them to get support, outgrow their comfort zones, and pursue their passions. Meetup is great for introverts. There will be a group to suit your interests. This app is a great place to meet women and people in general. I've met some women on there. I don't attend these meetups for that reason, but it's something I find myself doing. What can you say but I love women! I love women. LOL. I once met a woman in a polyamorous group that I was a part of and ended up hooking up with her. She was fascinating in a good way. But that's another story.

However, it doesn't mean that you have to wait to start dating online. You can do some self-improvement while you are online and I guarantee you will find success with women. In no time, you'll find beautiful women to date. Keep trying, be persistent and patient. You may not get any responses for the first few weeks. However, I can guarantee you that once you start getting dates you will have many to choose from. The "universe" opens up to you and sends them all your way. You will vibrate at a new frequency. That's my opinion.

Why Some Men Make It Harder

The number one reason that online dating fails for men is because they give up too early. They think that as soon as they set up a profile, they'll see immediate results. However, this is not true. It could take weeks, weeks, or even months to get results if you don't take action. If you haven't seen any results after two weeks of taking action, it is time to update the profile and give it a test. Another reason why men fail is that they keep trying different things and expecting different results. If you don't believe me, that's what defines insanity! If you try a strategy or technique but are not seeing the results you want, you need to modify it and test it again! Another reason that men sometimes get upset is this: These men cannot take any insult. If a neurotic woman makes a mean statement, it can have a devastating effect on your relationship. It doesn't matter what she thinks or speaks!

The Setup

This section will provide all the information you need for setting up your online dating profile. Yes! Multiple dating apps and sites, at minimum 3 in your local area. You can maximize your chances of meeting someone by creating profiles on several dating apps and sites. For the most part. At the time I write this, "Bumble" is my favorite. The app is free for Android and IOS users. Bumble lets you swipe right to indicate that you like someone. If you don't, swipe left. Bumble lets you swipe unlimited times, but the women need to message before you can message. The women have 24 hour to message before you remove them from your timeline.

Bumble is one of my favorites because of the great quality of women I find. Most are independent and beautiful women with great careers. I've had great interactions with the women on Bumble.

In fact, I met one of my current girlfriends on this app. OKC (Ok Cupid), my second favorite. This site is more like traditional dating websites and it's free to use. Here, you can message any woman that you like. Tinder is my third favorite. Tinder is the "hookup apps", but lets be honest, you'll find women on every dating app and site that want to "hookup", even on "Christian Mingles". Yes! Christian Mingles!

Tinder is also available for free, just like Bumble. Once you've liked her you can message and swipe. Keep in mind that Tinder is not like Bumble. You only get 100 swipes to "Likes" and then you must wait 12 hour before you can start swiping again for 'Likes' unless your sign up for the Membership offer. You have many choices, and I never sign up to any paid offers. But they do work. If you're interested in trying it, there are plenty of options. Tinder has many nice women.

Keep in mind that women on these dating sites can be from different areas. Set up profiles on various sites to see which ones have more quality women. Be careful with dating apps and websites. Many are full of fake profiles and filled with prostitutes and escorts. Don't be fooled!

Setting up Your Profile

Keep it brief, at most two paragraphs. This will allow you to be concise and direct about who you are. If you are seeking a serious relationship or marriage, be more detailed but keep it under three sentences. You've probably heard that a long, detailed profile will give you the best results. But let's face facts, women can become tired after reading through several lengthy profiles. This is why they tend to skim through the many thousands of profiles from men. Your "About Me", or "long life" bio is no longer as effective. Women are getting bombarded more often with messages. As a result, their attention span is much shorter. If they don't like what you have to say, they will quickly skim your profile. Next, make sure you check all applicable categories. A minimum of three photographs should be taken of you. One of you should be wearing a business outfit and one of you engaged in some sort of physical activity (gymn, CrossFits, jiu–jitsu or boxing). One picture of you with your friends doing some kind of sport or having fun (at a gym, rock climbing, in a lounge, concert etc.). These are the best types of pictures. However, if they are not possible, any pictures can be used. Be sure to update all your photos as soon as you can. Although I have found that pictures of you and other women in the photo don't work as well as they used too, I recommend you keep them up for testing. It doesn't matter what method you use to take the photos, just ensure that they are good quality. Many men are not willing to put in the effort or take enough photos, and they're missing out on possible dates with attractive ladies.

Please smile a big, genuine smile. Enough to show your teeth at the least in one of these pictures. I lost track how many women said "I was a little nervous about replying because you couldn't see my teeth in your photographs." You may have some missing teeth. The difference was huge when I included a photo with a real smile showing my teeth. Keep your "selfies" to a minimum. Two selfies is the maximum. Keep them at a minimum, two selfies max. A gym selfie is acceptable unless you are in great shape or showing your progress. Pictures of material items such as cars, money, your fancy house, and expensive watches are not allowed. It is a sign of being a tyrant and incompetent. You will attract only materialistic, sexy women. They will not appreciate you as a person. If you don't care that women want you only for your stuff and are just looking for sex, post photos of your lavish lifestyle. This will help you attract the type of woman you want.

Rotate the main picture every now and again. You will see better results with some photos than others. If you are in good physical shape, show off a picture of yourself without a shirt. Do not be discouraged if women complain about it. Many women love it. While some apps and websites allow you to upload shirtless photos as your profile picture, others may not. This is why it's important that you test it. These phones can take great quality pictures. Get some pictures taken of you by someone else and then upload them to your profile. It is possible to hire a professional photographer

(Recommended but not essential), as they will be able to take photos from various angles. You can find very affordable photographers on craigslist.org. For all your profiles on various dating apps and sites, you can use the exact same setup. My profiles all look identical. All the information is the same: pictures, "About Me", etc. You can use positive words in the "About me" section to describe yourself. Such words as self-motivated. success-driven. risk-taker. adventurer. caring. family-oriented. trustworthy. honest. loyal. great sense of humor. You get the point. These are qualities that women want in a man. These characteristics can be put in your own words and you can add more if needed. They look something like the one I've shown above. Be positive, and especially not negative about former girlfriends. You can also be funny. Based on your results, you can test and adjust your profile.

Chapter 11: The Nature of the Dating World and The Current State

The world of dating is complicated. It's full of different types and mazes. Contrary to what experts may have told you, women are complex and diverse creatures with different tastes. There is no magic formula for women and dating. When it comes to women, one approach is not as effective as another. There will always be new factors that can change your game. There are many factors to consider when dating. You should be able recognize these before you make your move.

You must consider the age of women. There are many factors that affect women's interests. A lot of girls find it easy to fall for a handsome man with a lovely smile. Her tastes change as she gets older. After a while, her taste in men changes and she will now only choose men who have the right attitude, social status, wealth, or wealth. Many women pick men based on their age once they reach a certain stage in life. For example, women older than 30 years are more likely to date well-educated men. You will be able to determine the right man for you by looking at the age range of women.

Also, consider what their tastes are in men. Many women prefer to date the athletic, teenage-aged type. Other women prefer the sophisticated man. There are macho women and those who love the Casanova romantic type. Some men prefer rugged, mustachioed men. Women have different preferences in terms of their tastes. Many of their tastes are influenced largely by the guys they've dated in the past, while some others are influenced more by their psychology. No matter your reasons for dating, it is important to recognize that women have different tastes.

Social status is important. Many women don't care whether you're wealthy or poor but they are more likely to choose richer men. Why do women tend to look at men's pockets before they are committed? Genetic factors play a role in this. Take the alpha-male factor. Alpha males in cavemen are considered the strongest of the tribe. After several centuries, power was not just measured in strength but also by wealth and fame. Since the most powerful men provide security, they are likely to be the ones chosen by women. Power is attractive. This is why social status matters.

You should also consider where you live when looking for love. It is common to choose different approaches to dating women depending on their location. If a woman asks for a drink, it is a good idea to do so. A woman may be allowed to have a drink in the bar. However, if you ask her for one in a library or supermarket, it will likely get laughed at. It is important to think about where you are going to approach women.

Location can have a big impact on the mood of your date. If you want to be serious but also get to know the girls better, it is impossible to do this in a noisy bar. When you're in a noisy bar, it can be difficult to be romantic. It is important to take into account your location when approaching women.

You now know what factors can affect your love life, so make sure to keep them in mind when you approach someone. These dating experts will tell you that their methods can be applied anywhere and to any person. It is up to them if they believe you. Be aware that there are always variables that can change your approach.

Chapter 12: Your Texting Game

If you can text a woman effectively, it can make her more attracted than she already seems. The difference between a man and a woman can be made by having a great texting skill. You can get women to be more attracted to your message if you follow the same steps as starting a conversation. The goal of texting is to take her out.

I am assuming you have at least one conversation using the above-described method. Your texting game is divided into two parts: the messages you send, and the sub-communication. The exact word choices and text length you use in the texts you send are what you will see in the messages you send. Sub-communication can be described as an indirect form or texting. You could, for example, reply to her texts every 5 second, even if it is 3 in the morning. This sub-communication tells her that you have no existence.

Send a text to a woman no later than two days after you have received her number. Do not leave it longer than that, as she will gradually lose interest. If you wait more than 10 minutes to talk, the attraction she has for you will fade. Perhaps you are wondering what examples of good first text messages would work. To begin with, don't use "Hey" or any other similar words in your first text. This doesn't stimulate any of the girl's emotions and it is a terrible way to start a message. One good example is:

Hey [insert nickname here], it was great to talk to you at the [insert locale here]! Your [insert interest here] was fascinating to me.

This text means more to her than the text "hey", as it conveys that you enjoyed your conversation with her, and that she was interested in your interests. Be gentle with her when texting. Keep texting using these three techniques: Stimulate her emotion, unpredictable texts, pulling back. You can stimulate her emotions by sending positive texts. Never compliment her body or appearance with texts. You should not send her unpredicted texts. Unpredictable texts include texts that have a different length, word choice or emojis. This isn't too difficult, but it's worth remembering to mix it up a little. An emoji can be used in text messages. Some texts may allow for a longer message, while others will allow for a shorter version. This is not complicated. Third, and most importantly, pull out of the conversation. This is an effective way to get her to be more interested in you. Stopping the conversation means that you stop to text her while she is talking. This sounds silly, but it really is incredible. Consider this:

You have been texting the woman for 2 days straight. If she asks you a question, or makes a statement that you normally reply to, you can pull out of the conversation. This is because she will be left wondering about you, your activities and why you suddenly stopped responding. Your attractiveness is immediately increased. Let's say you were on the other end. You are in a relationship, and you text your woman daily. The conversation suddenly ends and she stops responding to your messages for the next couple hours. You will think about what she is doing and how she got there. You will now be more attracted her. You will also find unpredictability (pulling aside from conversations) attractive as it shows that you're not like everyone else. The relationship status affects the time that you choose to walk away. The three components of relationship status are: you have only met one woman; you've had 2-4 dates with women looking to start a romance; and you are currently in a relationship. The more men text, the closer you become to one another. In this situation, you can pull away for only a few hours. But if you are on only three to four dates, you can pull away for a longer amount of time. Short story: The more intimate your relationship is, then the less you talk. This will not have any effect. You should not use this technique more than three times a day. She will quickly get used and become predictable.

Chapter 13: Dealing with Rejection

Rejection can be one of most painful aspects of your attractiveness journey. People feel that the world is closing down when they are rejected. They fail to see the good that lies behind rejection. I've been rejected many times in my life. I was insecure because I didn't know how confidence works. It was because I failed the lesson that rejection tried to teach. I blame the girls instead and claim that it is their fault that I was rejected.

I did have some bad rejections. This was especially before Models, the book that taught me how I could be more attractive. My rejections were mostly due to my inability to communicate with girls, and the time I spent talking to them. I never met a girl facetoface. I used test them for

3-4 week and then asked them if they would consider being my girlfriend.

This was a mistake. The social media world isn't social. Making a girl your boyfriend via social media is difficult and takes away from the fun of the dating process. It can feel great to be rejected, as you will see. Let me explain. Arnold used the saying that for every positive change in your life there will be a painful one. The people who make it work are the ones who get through the pain. You can't avoid the pain if you want success.

Let's now get back to my story. After years spent being rejected and lacking emotional connections, I finally realized that I needed help. I purchased a book called Models. It changed my life. In fact, it is a combined resume of Models plus my personal experiences. After finishing that book, I began working out and noticed a difference in my body. Also, my beard grew. This added another benefit to my look. The moment I finally got a girl to like me was here, I knew it was my moment.

The first two days were not successful. I searched for pretty girls, but could not find one that would suit my needs. The 3 days that I stayed at the hotel, I was walking along the road and saw a sweet girl on a bench. I was walking with a friend and decided to walk to the hotel in order to get him. I met her again after that. I needed to be more confident because this was the first time I did it. So I walked down, then back up. I looked at her for a second and then decided to follow her. It was too late, so I held out my hand and introduced me. After that, she introduced herself to me and told me her name was Andreea. We spend hours talking and meeting one another.

Evidently, she was looking for her cousin who was missing. So she came to the club along with me. We danced, talked, and then she asked me if I would come to her home. She wanted to wear something more formal, so I agreed. We had a great time. I was too strict and wanted to leave. She spent too much of her time on her phone. Although it's nice to have high standards it's equally important to be able and willing to overlook minor issues. I could tell her that it upsets me, which would have been the right decision. I told her I wanted to leave, and she said she regretted it. She requested that I stay at least until her cousin arrives. Seeing that I am getting bored, she took my hands and took me to dance. After we left, she asked me to go back to my hotel. She was scared so I did not kiss her. Tomorrow was the worst day of my life. I regretted it when she sent me a text saying she loves me and feels terrible that she must leave. She would have liked a chance to meet me.

Although it didn't turn out as I expected, it was an important moment in my journey. It was the first time that a really cute girl was really interested in me. All that I did was to meet her (risk rejection), then present myself as rawly as possible. Three nights later, confident, ready to meet a girl, I went to the club. I danced, did some photos, and laughed with friends. As I was dancing, I saw a beautiful girl with her friend. Because of the success I had previously achieved, I got up and braved myself to go into her room. She was not interested in me, so I approached her friend. So I could go meet her and then move on to my second business. But I had to wait for the girls that were not interested in me to tell me before I could give my hand to the girl I was most interested in.

"But... But... Ouch, it was hard to leave but I wasn't mad at all.

My confidence was higher. At least, it wasn't wasted. I knew that I am attractive, and that I would find someone that makes me happy. As evidence, six months later I fell in love with my current girlfriend. We are as happy together as two can be.

Do not view rejection as a defeat. Instead, remember that 90% of people will wait months or even years before saying something only to be rejected. You don't waste your time if you move quickly. Even if you're rejected, learn from it and move on.

Today, my rejections represent the milestone of my attraction. Without a rejection of a girl I really liked in highschool, I would not have read Models. And my relationship would have been miserable.

This concludes this chapter. Do not be afraid of rejection. It is part and parcel of the dating process. If you are rejected, don't worry. You will learn from it. Then, move on. Nobody can judge how wonderful you are but you. You have to believe in yourself. I know I do.

Chapter 14: Making Ageless Love Last

The Permanent Partnership

I enjoy hearing stories about couples that make their relationships last. I'm not referring to those who live in harmony, but those who share a deep, eternal love for each others. They were my dad's and mom's parents. I can recall a night that passed not too long before my dad died. He was in the hospital. A nurse called my mom's house at close to midnight. She was my companion. We both panicked at the possibility that something had happened to him in such an unusual hour. When I handed the phone back to my mom, I felt a relief as I saw a gentle smile spread across her tired face. My eyes were able to see her transformation into a young girl full of joy, full of love and giggles. I've never seen anything quite like it. Soon, I learned that my dad was very passionate about my mother and shared his love with his nurse. He even retold their entire story about how they met. It was at their wedding. My mother ran straight up to my father at the bar, while he was still thinking about it. With a little flirty humour, she said "I knooow yours!" This was an amazing and brave move. Her delightful manner let him catch her. They danced throughout the night. He refused to let another man enter. Dad told the nurse how his mom was afraid to accept his marriage proposal, as he was eleven-months younger. The story was something I had heard many times, but never like this. It was so beautiful, and so romantic that the nurse felt an urge to call mom right away. Mom recalls often the phone call that Dad made to her that night, even though Dad has since passed. Her smile is the same as his sincere love for her. It would have been so tragic if she didn't take the leap of faith to try and make her marriage work with a younger man. That was in 1940s America, when even a year was considered an age. You should not let the age you love stop you from loving your partner.

These secrets will lead to a happy partnership between you, your Boy Toy. You can never lose sight of the fact that it is never too late.

The Trust Bond - Honesty, Loyalty, and Treasure

Honesty, loyalty, and trustworthiness are the best investments for the future of your relationship.

Honesty

You are likely to have been raised to value honesty as a high virtue, especially as a hot BTB. How mature woman can forget the "Honest Abe" role model? Boy Toys believe that Abe the good old man is an excuse to shop at Best Buy every February. They have been raised in an environment that allows dishonesty to be accepted as part of society. Therefore, if you think he deserves your love, you may need to teach him the importance of honesty. He should be taught the value of sharing secrets, stories, and any other information with you. He must know that honesty can only lead to trust. I insist on telling the truth, even if that hurts. Let him be aware that any lie, by omission or otherwise, is forbidden. These are just that, lies. Your Boy Toy may tell you that he has never had sex but he actually participated in oral sexual pleasure. Both of you have to find a way to create a safety zone where you can both express what you want without attacking each other. He will be open to your honesty.

It does not give you a pat for your head simply because you tell the truth.

However, it does not excuse the wrongdoing. Many feel that admitting guilt should save them from any emotional turmoil. Don't be ashamed! Because it is the right thing, you should tell the truth.

Trust

Boy Toys frequently tell me that older women become jealous too easily. They don't know why you feel that way. They think you are hot. Most of the time, it's not a problem. You shouldn't expect to be able to see your partner every second of every day. That's where trust comes into play. Trust means you don't have to keep checking in. Perhaps it's time for you to put aside your age differences and have faith that your Boy Toy will be there. But if trust is broken it can be very difficult for them to restore their relationship. The guidelines for a relationship can change. You need to regain your trust in him if you are caught cheating. He should allow you to monitor him. This can provide temporary comfort. It's a great thing if he makes it a point to prove that he is yours only. If trust is restored, you can ask him for more frequent calls or to do whatever it takes. These older women often feel jealous. It's because you naturally get jealous when you see him lie to you. This can increase your need to be reassured constantly, which he may come to dislike. It is his fault to allow you to be called "jealousy". Your "jealousy" feelings should not be attributed to your age. This is not jealousy. It's more about a lack in trust. Take it back!

Cyndi's Secrets(tm)

We are always told to forgive and forget. Forgiving is great. You should never forget. For example, if your younger male abuses you, be kind and forgive him. However, do not forget. Get help!

Loyalty

Loyalty shows that you can count upon each other. Loyalty is about trusting your partner. It's okay for older men to cheat as long they are loyal to their wives. They often mistake loyalty for being the financial provider. Younger men seem more to recognize the difference between loyalty or trust. Maybe it's because Boy Toys tend to make less money than BTBs. Click on Webster.com to review the terms with your partner, before you make a commitment.

Communication

Let's examine how good communication skills can help you make a lasting partnership with a younger gentleman. These are some of our top tips.

* You both need to pay attention. Boy Toys sometimes shout and get angry during fights. He might feel that it is his

primal right and right as a male. To be fair, you might view him as immature, or you may shout even louder. You shout and yell at him, and then we all shout "You'ren't listening!" It could be that he or she is not really listening or cannot accept that there are different opinions. Many relationships can be saved by learning to listen. To be able to listen, it's important to acknowledge that sometimes disagreeing is acceptable. One of the shining lights in my study is the unanimous praise for Boy Toys' listening skills by the women. BTMs taught their sons well.

* Don't interrupt. Ladies, I hate it to say this, but sometimes some guys have trouble with dealing with the conversation without taking a deep breath between sentences. Your Boy Toy should stop talking and allow you to speak. He is much more mature than you and cares about your opinions. He will do anything to get

your thoughts out, so he can listen to what you have to share. You don't have to worry about him interrupting your work. Boy Toys tend not to interrupt as much as older men. Two voices are needed to make a partnership work.

* Don't listen to just what you want. Boy Toys may not be able to handle an entire argument. They are fast to move on to the next topic and are very young. Because of this, they may not hear everything they need to hear. This is because they are often able to communicate quickly thanks to texting, instant messaging (IMs) and sound bites. While hot BTBs can also be high-tech but many of us grew up without it. For us, the transition between an in-depth conversation or a Nextel moment can be easier. Boy Toys love to listen and will not be offended if you ask them. You should also listen to the "message" behind Boy Toys' words.

* Your partner should not be talking while you plan your next sentence. BTBs are often guilty. Your younger man may grow impatient and become frustrated. Boy toys don't have the same life experience as you. Your cognitive ability may be stronger. This doesn't necessarily mean you are better, but it does indicate that you have gone through a phase that he has yet to complete. Give him the space to gather his thoughts, and give him 100 percent of your attention. It is disrespectful to be rehearsing his lines while he is speaking. It is normal for him to be attentive to your words.

* Repeat what your partner just said. It allows your partner to know that you are paying attention. This is classic communication. It transcends generations and genders. It is a process that can be repeated until both of you are able to understand the thoughts of the other.

* You should not reply with your belief until you understand what your partner meant. Your belief may be more mature than his because he's younger. He might believe that your thoughts have become outdated. The two of them must make a mature decision to put aside the age excuses. Only then can each of you really understand what the other is thinking, make a respectful response, and then come up with a resolution--together!

Touching

After we have discussed communication, let us now discuss touching. From friendship to a long-lasting relationship, intimacy is achieved through touch. It could be the gentle touch on a shoulder or a kiss at a mall. Or hot, steamy sex in the rain on Saturday afternoon. A Boy Toy and a Girl Toy are likely to be better matched sexually than if they were together with a woman their age or you with an older guy.

Touch can go beyond the sexual. A relationship can last forever if it is the union between your mind, body and spirit. Being kind to one another is vital. It makes it so much easier when you are physically matched!

Humor

Laughter makes the best medicine. Sometimes, generational gaps affect how each person thinks funny. You might laugh out loud at classic Laughin episodes. Your Boy Toy likely doesn't have a complete understanding of the history and humor behind the show. There are gender differences. Although I never understood humor, most guys love it. But this doesn't mean you have to give up on the younger man. Humor is more than telling jokes. Humor can be about celebrating the good in life and looking forward to the positive side. You can go from fighting to laughing and hugging with your friends by sharing a common humor--sharing positive, funny, and fresh takes on life.

Respect

A relationship is one where both partners are respectful and supportive of one another. Boy Toys is very conscious of this. I interviewed a Boy Toy aged 30 last night. He couldn't stop talking about how much he loved the way his BTB believed in him. He is confident that he can accomplish anything because of her. His past relationships with younger women left him feeling depressed and not good enough. Hot BTBs require respect. You can't beat a dose of admiration from a younger gentleman who looks up to your accomplishments and, most importantly, your personality. Respect means working as a team but also accepting and supporting one another. You can let your younger man know that you are proud that he did his best and makes less than you. These are some suggestions to help you ensure respect.

No Games

I hate playing games. It's childish. Don't do it! Hot BTBs often make age their trump card. As a result, you're more skilled. This allows you to be manipulative or abusive. Consider this: You don't want Boy Toy to return to college, because you are afraid he might meet someone of the same age. Instead of telling him the truth, it is possible to go into a song and dance routine about how much he would waste his time. Or worse, you could tell him that he doesn't know enough. It might feel great to get your way but it is totally disrespectful. He shouldn't play games, except maybe Twister with you.

Who is the First to Go?

Respect for one another is only possible if you put your partner first. This will help you achieve an amazing balance in your relationship. It is common for one partner to give more than another. This is common in relationships with older men. Boy Toys are often eager to please. They will often put you first, for the most parts. They look up and admire you for your individuality and success. It is important to tell your younger man that you are the most important person in your life.

Boy Toy Talk

"He was nine years younger than me, but still respected me and my successes." He was proud that I was well-known in my field. Since I was already working when we met, there was no competition between us. When I consider the amount of self-confidence he must've had to approach and approach me, it is obvious that he was exceptional. Most men were competitive or intimidated. I appreciated his level of respect for me. I didn't have to fight for it."

Fighting Fair

A relationship that is long-term can be expected to reveal the things that could make your Boy Toy vulnerable. It is a sign of respect that you will not give your Boy Toy this information in a fight. Let's say a younger man climbs the ladder of success, but isn't quite there yet. It would be cruel of him to be called a total Marilyn, 60 loser in an unrelated fight. It's unfair for him to shout out in spite, "nobody want an old hag as you." But it is better not to attack one another. Stay focused on the issues. Fight fair!

The Last Word

It is not always important to have the final word in a loving marriage. This is something hot BTBs must remember. Let's face truth: We are often confident and strong and like to have our own way. These are all good traits, but you need to protect your young man from these qualities. Your Boy Toy should also respect you. There are many things that seem insignificant in the grand scheme. It can help strengthen your relationship by allowing yourself to give in or letting go on occasion. You can let go of the unnecessary stuff.

It's never too late

Maybe you believe you are too old or too young to be in a loving relationship with someone younger than you really are. Gretchen, Walter and I had the chance to interview them recently. Here's their story.

Gretchen didn't even think about the possibility of being in her 70s. She was too busy planning for her future. When her husband of 42-years died suddenly, Gretchen had to find a way back into her life. Gretchen felt lost and alone. They loved their Michigan home. Her two sons had grown up and she was no longer surrounded by her family. She decided to sell their house and move into an apartment. Gretchen was left with the responsibility of picking up the pieces after her husband's death. After allowing herself to grieve, she decided that it was finally time for her to take control of her life at 72. She got a job with Burger King.

Being a hostess was a wonderful way to get out of her head and be with people. She enjoyed talking with customers. One stood out. Walter was his real name. Walter was a charming gentleman with a quirky personality that women loved and admiration from men. He was friendly and he always made her smile every time he entered. He was a friendly man, and she could sense his deep sadness. Gretchen discovered that Walter's spouse and two of his children died within minutes of each another. He was feeling the weight of his loneliness, no matter how much he tried to conceal it.

Chapter 15: Ace The First Date

A woman does not need to be taken to expensive restaurants on her first date. The first date can be likened to a foundation for your entire courtship. The first date allows you to get to know your partner and determine if she is your ideal woman. Keep things simple.

Once I took a woman out on a first date. We went to a very expensive restaurant for dinner. As the evening went on, I realized that I was always the one talking. It was so boring, I felt like it was a waste of my time and money to invite her over.

She didn't have any interest in me. Her primary concern was her phone, and not me as her dinner companion. As you can see in my case, I took her with me to an expensive restaurant. We had a terrible evening. I never asked her out again after the date. That was also the last time she spoke to me.

You don't have to accept a woman going out on a first date to make her feel comfortable. You might find that you dislike the woman on your first date. Do not be overly extravagant on your first date.

10.1. Where to Take Her on a First Date

For your first date, take her to these locations - it's a great place to take her.

A nice coffee shop

A good restaurant

Bowling

A nice park

An art museum

A bar (or outdoor bars)

You want to enjoy conversation, laughter, and having fun with your partner. Do not take her on your first date to the movies and cinemas. You shouldn't take your girlfriend to the movies or loud music venues. Talking is a great way to build trust and intimacy. You should only take your first date with her to a place that you can talk, so you can learn as much about her as you can. You can always have fun later. Imagine you're dating five girls. Each girl must be taken to expensive venues.

Be a gentleman

It's important to be punctual for your date, and to keep the car door open for her. She should open her car door. Be a gentleman to pick her up and meet her at the door.

Be kind to her and give her a compliment. Remark on how beautiful she looks. Be proud of the fact that she has taken the time to dress up. You can compliment her, but don't go overboard. I normally compliment a woman after I pick her up. Don't overdo it on compliments. This will come off as unauthentic or as a bribe to sex.

I had mentioned in our conversations that if a woman has a negative perception of you, it is very difficult to date her. I have made so many stupid compliments.

I vividly remember video chatting with a woman. I told her that she is beautiful and she replied, "Thank you." Later in the conversation, she said that I was "wow". You've already said that to me.

Beautiful and attractive women are particularly sensitive to the idea of a man only being interested in their physical appearance. Most successful men also hate it when a woman only is interested in his money. This has been the case with many beautiful ladies. If she feels that this man likes me only because of my appearance, she will likely reject you. Make sure you are careful when giving compliments.

Don't make things too complicated

In general, men tend to complicate the dating process. The process is simple. Just be yourself and do minimal work, and things will happen naturally. The best relationship you could have with a woman is one that flows naturally. This is a relationship in which she loves you for your uniqueness and you love her because of it.

Be yourself on your first date. Do not start out telling lies. It will only backfire. To build a solid, healthy relationship with your partner, you must first lay the foundation. You can find many women that bring you immense joy. The saying "behind all great men is an amazing woman" is true. However, it can be very rewarding to have a woman in the life of your dreams.

Women can spot your blind spots as much as you are able to see them. A woman who encourages you can push you to your full potential. You will get the best out of a woman that is good to you. I've known friends who weren't careful with their appearances and didn't care about themselves. However, once they had a girlfriend, my eyes began to see the positive changes. Many began to keep their homes clean and dressed well. Some men even started managing their finances well, while others began to take their business seriously and pursue a career.

Keep the conversation light and positive

It is essential to have a positive and light conversation on your first date. Keep it lighthearted and playful. Women love to have fun and feel relaxed when out. Have a great time on your first date.

You will be the leader of the conversation so avoid talking about negative topics. Do not tell her about the hardships or sufferings you have been through. Attracting a woman to you is not possible if she feels sorry for her. It doesn't help to make her feel sorry about yourself.

For women, masculine strength is appealing. A woman is attracted to a strong male partner. If you are going out with a woman, you will want to be the one leading. She will want you as the one who tells her where to meet her and what to do with her. However, while most women want to be submissive and obedient to their man, the sad fact is that most men are not fulfilling their masculine role.

Asking a woman to tell you where they should meet is a common response. Let her lead.

Women are happy to submit to a strong, focused man. A woman often boasts to her friends that she can say, "Hey, take a look!" This is my guy." If a woman feels your masculine energy and strength, she will automatically feel her feminine energy. Feminine energie is about allowing yourself to be loved, connected, and shared with others.

A woman's purpose is to have a man. All women desire to be loved, appreciated, cherished, and respected. Sometimes a woman will contact your office after she hasn't heard back from you for a while to let her know you are still there. If a woman dresses up in makeup, has her hair done, and wears well-made clothes, it is most likely to be doing so to gain appreciation from the men. Your wife may dress up in a beautiful outfit or put on a great outfit for you.

The man she is with is likely to fail if a woman doesn't take care of herself or is too bitchy. Did you ever see a woman reject a man of wealth or fall in love? Because the financially less fortunate man understands women, and is likely a master at making them feel loved.

When you first meet someone, it is important that she does most of the talking. You will likely talk your woman out of liking you if you talk too much.

Let her do the most of all the talking

Your first and subsequent dates should have the woman doing 70-80% talking. It is important to ask questions. Women love it when a man takes an interest in her and is willing to answer all of their questions. Sometimes, when I end a date and meet a woman, I will hear her say "I don't really know anything about you" or "you haven't talked much about yourself." This can make a second date very likely.

It is a good thing for a woman that you are the one finding out information. If she is curious about your partner, that shows her romantic interest. If you're in a relationship, don't divulge any personal information. Men who talk too much about themselves during a date are likely to lose their attraction. The woman will see it as a deflection on who you are as someone and say, "He looks needy, insecure, and uncertain of himself."

One of my friends has a great relationship with women. He shared stories with me about having sex while he was unknown to women. It won't make her love you more if you tell her all your successes or failures. Focus on the conversation and let her do the talking. Find out as many details as you possibly can about her. The person asking the questions controls the conversation.

Mindfully handle past relationships and sex conversations

Sometimes, a woman may openly discuss her past relationships with you or ask you questions about yours. Be respectful of her ex-boyfriends and partners. A woman's intuition has a lot of power. Women are very good at reading body language and how it is spoken. Attractivity can be killed by what you say.

It is important to avoid bringing up sex during your first date, even if she brings it up. Most women go out with men on the second or threerd date, except if she is religious, rule-governed or structured. Some women will even share a bed with men on the first date.

Sex is something that women desire, but it depends on how they are treated. Many women don't like it when you only desire sex from them. You should not talk about sex too often and switch the topic at the first natural opportunity. Most women have had to deal with men who dump them after having sex.

Sex shouldn't be an issue if a woman sees that you are genuine interested in her, pass all her tests and are a man. She will readily give you sex if you don't make it a priority. If you are so attached to her vagina that you allow it to control you, then you won't get any sex.

Take her to multiple places

Take her to several venues or places on your first date. This gives you multiple opportunities to have fun with her. To start the date, take her to a nice restaurant, café, or park. Spend around 45 minutes to 1 hours there. Then, go to another spot that offers something more, such as bowling, darts, etc.

Always be the one to end your dates. You don't need to spend so much time with her on your first meeting. You can keep it short and leave her wanting more. You can keep it short and let her have fun. She will want to know when you plan on going out again. It's always better for the woman to bring up the idea about meeting and going out. If she is following you, it is not abandoning you. A woman asking you to go out is interested. If she opens the door, you just need to go through it.

Sometimes a woman might show an obvious interest in someone, but the man may not be able see it. The man pursues her even though she expressed an interest in him. It is okay to show interest in a woman, but you don't need to pursue it. All you have to do is reciprocate. If she suggests that you go out with her, or get together, schedule a date and then call her. You don't need to be calling her daily. Setting dates with her once or twice per week should be your priority. When she falls in love, she will always want to be there for you.

You can escalate things

It is important to escalate the situation so you don't become a friend zoned woman. When you first meet someone, make sure to touch, hug, and hold hands with her. If you touch, hug or hold hands with the woman, it shows that you aren't afraid of her. It makes you more comfortable. Goodnight kisses on the lips are a great way to end a first date. If you're interested in a woman, she'll kiss you back.

If she doesn't turn her head when you approach her cheek, that is an indication she doesn't have a romantic interest. This point is when you know that she doesn't want to go out again with you. I generally give a woman three dates. I ask her to be open with me after this.

Only spend time or date with women who are highly attracted to your personality. After giving her your good night kiss, you can say "I had an enjoyable time" or "It has been a pleasant evening." But don't go into detail! Remain in the center of your attention and leave her to wonder about how great a time it was.

Remind her to consider whether she was successful or not. Next, ask her to replay the date with her mind and review all the clues. You will not give her the solution. You will remain a mystery. Your attraction level to her is growing as she thinks about you and the date.

After the kiss, you should leave. You're going to leave her confused. It is a scientific fact, that women feel more attracted towards men whose feelings remain ambiguous.

You should always be prepared for a place to take a woman on a date. You should always remember that a woman who is interested and in you romantically will want to sex. However, you have to initiate sex in order for it to take place. If you wait too long, another man can take your place.

Before you go out with your girlfriend, ensure you have a space where you can share time. If you don't have your space, you can make arrangements to rent a hotel room. Some women don't like the idea of staying in a hotel.

You can also travel to her home but it is risky. Some women you date may have "undisclosed" boyfriends. This could create problems if you are found together. Some men pay the rent to their girlfriends. Can you imagine the consequences if a man is paying his girlfriend's rent and finds out she is cheating? Is this not how crimes committed in passion are made?

Get your expectations right

You shouldn't be thinking about what you can get from any relationship. To give, you should enter a relationship. It is easier to get hurt when you focus on giving than receiving. Emotional harm is usually caused by unmet expectations.

Sometimes a woman will reject your proposal, but later realize her mistake and make a comeback. This is quite common, especially if things went right. It's important to always make your time together a positive one. This is how you must approach all relationships and women in your lives. Have fun, be playful, and remain confident and grounded. When you do these things, you will attract the woman that you want.

Chapter 16: Remain The Man Of Her Dreams

You can learn any skill best by breaking it down into smaller pieces and working on each part. Talking with women is nothing but a learned skill, as you've seen in this book. That is what you should do with this book.

Truth is that you'll learn a lot faster than you expected once you really get into it. Every component of communication is something you want to focus on. In case you don't already know the story, Ben Franklin created a list of virtues that he believed he should improve.

He had 3x5 cards and wrote virtues on each one. Every day, he would get one of his 3x5 cards and try to improve that virtue. As he continued to live his life, he discovered that he actually improved his virtues.

Each day, pick one of these elements and work on improving it. You will find that your skills are improving day by day. As your brain wires for these abilities, you will be able to combine innuendo and humor, as well as storytelling and nonverbal communication.

This is the great news! It is possible to do it because everything is already in place. This awareness will make you more aware of how communication works and allow you to communicate clearly with others. You can make adjustments until you get the results that you want.

You now understand that you can evaluate and manage your own communication. It's something that very few men know or do. You can rise above it and make it work. When men engage in conversation with women, they are often fully engaged in the conversation. They aren't evaluating it. There are no mental processes. They are simply talking. They're totally in the moment.

It is important to understand that you can always change the outcome of communication once you have started learning it and getting better at storytelling.

Very few men are aware that the brain of a human being is capable of doing this. They are blindly following cars, just going from one statement to the next.

They may get lucky and catch one every now and then. The man goes out to meet women and hopes that they will be attracted to him.

Now you're clear that this is nothing to do with luck. This is a science-based skill. You can learn it, so you don't have to be a genius to do this.

Literally, you can choose any woman that you wish.

If you're trying to tie everything together and switch between all the forms of communication, stimulating different areas of the female mind by different use of each of them, then you want to communicate, calibrate and pay attention. Based on the feedback you receive, you can modify or continue your communication. You are always aware about the impact of your communication on others.

It seems hard work at first. This is something that every good salesperson does. And every communicator knows how to do it naturally. You will soon be able to drive a car if you can think of it. Just think about it. It was scary when you first learned to drive a motor vehicle, or to ride a bicycle.

It is frightening to learn to drive. But, after you've completed the training, you will soon forget about it. It becomes a routine and a habit.

Pilots, helicopter pilots, fighter pilots all experience the same thing. Although they are learning to do the exact same thing in a complex machine, their consciousness fades into unconscious competence. It is important to consider all the mental processes you need to manage such a complex machine safely. Even though you are driving a car which is quite complex, you eventually get to the point that it disappears into the background.

Talking to women is simple, when compared to other things, and it's not difficult. You're having fun. You are looking at a gorgeous woman. There are only two or three things going on simultaneously. Your brain can handle them all.

There is no secret. You just learned to communicate, and you can use the communication that you already have. Communication which most men have never used or developed. The best thing about this is that you now have an edge. Now that you understand the communication strategies women use, you can start to practice them. They can be trained. You can improve their performance. They are possible to improve. These are things you can concentrate on.

Most men don't know that they can do it. Your brain is like muscle. You work your brain as hard as you can. It's the identical thing. You can quickly improve your skills by practicing via instant message chat.

You might start with one chat if you really want this stuff to be mastered. This is where you will work on innuendo. You can then open another chat and work on teasing, storytelling, or sarcasm. It's important to keep everything straight. It's a simulator. Talking to women in real life is the best thing in the world if your brain can handle it.

This is the way great NFL coaches have always done it. They make practice more difficult than the games so that the players feel relieved when they get to the game. However, to her it seems that you are quick-witted, which is very true.

Your mind will become faster the more you do this. And the faster you can create sarcasms, innuendos, teasing, and storytelling, the smarter women will see you. You may be surprised at the things that come out of you mouth.

You tell stories. She will be riveted by the analogies, word pictures, and witticisms. You communicate at a high level. Your subconscious brain is working at a high level and you may even be impressed with what you communicate.

Your subconscious mind absorbs all of this information. Your subconscious mind can take a while to process information and then you have to spit it all out. You may be learning something consciously, but it might take some time to process everything and make sense the next morning. Your subconscious mind is able to put it all together quickly.

It's from this place that the phrase "Let Me Sleep on it" is derived. Your subconscious will connect it and you'll get there. It will all happen by itself. It's easy to see the benefits of learning this stuff. Even if you are a good student, you will find that your subconscious mind is programming you better.

This is why this is so thrilling. You can quickly learn to communicate with women and gain a competitive edge over other men.

Because you have the funny stories, the witty replies, the innuendo, the humor, and the wit, women will feel more comfortable talking to you. Even if they're not with you, you'll notice that women suddenly respond to your presence.

Chapter 17: How to Overcome Online Dating Hurdles

This chapter addresses the most frequent online-dating problems and provides solutions.

Five single-parent dating problems

These are five single-parent dating challenges that are most prevalent and how to overcome them.

How to conquer a Hurdle

How do you know if your are ready? If you don't want to fulfill a void and you wish to be able to date, you might not be ready.

It is hard to find the time to give your children a good life and also to have a relationship. If you are open to dating, make sure you schedule your time. Invite your family and friends to babysit for you while you treat yourself on a date.

How much information should you share about your current circumstances? Even though it can add an element to the dating scene, being a single parent does not make you a criminal. It is not a crime to be single parent. It is important to be open and honest about what you are going through. There are many ways to find someone special, but being honest is the best way to do it.

Unsolicited, negative advice received from well-meaning family members and friends. Do not listen to anyone who tells you that single parents can't find love. Believe in yourself. Be confident that you can use online dating for your perfect partner.

How to tell the children about your exciting relationship. It is important that you take your time. Only tell the kids when you're confident in your relationship with your new "significant" other.

You should be able to conquer the most common single parent dating hurdles if you keep these tips in mind.

2: Online Romances with Long-Distance Partners

Yes, long-distance relationships may be difficult but with the right approach you can have a successful long-distance relationship.

Here are some common problems in long-distance relationships that can be overcome.

Hurdle How can you overcome it

Miscommunication/lack of

Open communication is the best method to overcome miscommunication. Do not suppress your emotions. Instead, discuss them with your partner.

Jealousy Accept the fact that it is normal to feel jealous, especially when your partner lives so far away. But don't allow the monster to overtake you. You can talk openly to your partner about how you feel, so that you can both work through it together.

Loneliness - Use modern technology to avoid feeling lonely in an online relationship. You can communicate with your partner frequently by video-chatting or calling at least once per day. The less lonely you feel, the more you can stay in touch with your partner.

Remember these obstacles and their solutions when you use online dating.

3: Unattractive/Not Good - Looking Enough

Online dating is very physical-appearance-driven because of the swiping nature of dating apps. This can prove to be a challenge if you are not confident or attractive.

Here are the most frequent dating challenges you may face if your feelings of unattractiveness or insufficient masculinity are revealed and how you can overcome them.

How to Overcome Hurdles

How to present your best "face", in your profile picture. A witty, yet honest photo is the best way to "put your best face forward". Do not attempt to photoshop beautiful faces onto your body. An action shot or a photograph that shows you fully immersed in something you are passionate about is unbeatable.

Your dating bio: What should you say about yourself? It's a space where you can express yourself authentically about who and what makes your heart sing. This space is a place to let women know what you stand for without sharing too much.

It is difficult to choose the right dating app. But, optimizing your dating profile will ensure that you find someone who truly loves you. Nerd Passions and Geek 2 Geek are two examples of niche dating sites that you can't go wrong.

Remember, beauty is in the eyes. You may not consider yourself attractive, but you will be beautiful to the right person. To find your dream girl, all you need to do is keep searching.

4: Dating problems for middle-aged men

If you're middle-aged, these are the common dating difficulties you will encounter and how you can solve them.

Hurdle How do you overcome it

It can be difficult to understand internet language and lingo. You need to be able speak the language of online dating. Google is your best friend if you find these words and others.

How to stay safe when using online dating. Middle-aged men (and ladies) are prime targets of scammers. To protect yourself from being scammed and keep your identity private, you should not give out personal information. You also need to be careful and attentive about what your matches are saying. Google can verify the information (even images) of your matches. It is safer than sorry.

Which dating app do you prefer? Any dating app can be used, but for the best results, it's best if you choose a dating app that is specifically designed for singles over 40 such as Lumen and OurTime.

These tips will help you to overcome the three most common problems that middle-aged couples face when dating.

How to Get Over Language Barriers in Online Dating

If you want to meet someone who speaks a different tongue, it will be difficult to overcome language barriers. Use online translators and apps to help you overcome any language barriers. Even if you only know a few words, it is the best way to get over them. You can also hire a translator. The most trusted intercultural dating platforms offer translation service.

Chapter 18: Be vulnerable and stop taking things too personally

Vulnerability, like power, allows you the freedom to express your inner essence and core. To be successful, you must not play small. It is not possible to be the person you were meant to be. If you hold on to your things and try to be someone someone else wants, you will not be happy.

Your goal should always be to feel at ease being yourself, indifferent and unaffected by whatever your dream lady throws at me. To be vulnerable, it means to be honest, to show your true feelings and not hide them. If you don't feel comfortable being vulnerable, you can't be in a love relationship with a woman. It is important to be vulnerable and express your love for her.

You might get rejected and your flaws or weaknesses exposed to her, but that is the beauty of being human. Demonstrating perfection can make you untrustworthy, and it can also make you look largely unreal. Be open to giving your woman the gift that is your genuine honesty. Don't let problems build up. Never allow any circumstance to stop you from your goals.

Be vulnerable and be prepared to receive rejection. If you are vulnerable, it is an opportunity to show who you really are. You don't want people to think you are someone you're not. In fact, if that happens, you will be forced to conform to your fake persona which will lead to immense pain. In all relationships, be honest enough to let others see you as you are.

If you are open and vulnerable, your emotions will be shared with those who matter. If they don't then you won't get along. You will have a difficult time being open with your partner. You will save years of time and heartache if you tell your partner and she ends the relationship.

Your vulnerability should be shared with all people. Be naked, and show your true self and your friends.

13.1: You shouldn't take things too personal

You don't have to take what a woman has to say or do personally. Sometimes women will test how strong you really are. You'll be surprised at how they react.

You'll struggle to find love and relationships if you are emotionally attached and sensitive to what women say or do. You should not take what a lady says to you seriously unless your love is deep and full at the moment she says it.

Sometimes, when she says "I hate," or "I don't want go to the movie theaters," it is often more a moment feeling than a thought-out experience. In most cases, though, men are not easily moved emotionally or by feelings. The masculine usually means what it says.

A man's word will be his honor. The feminine says what she feels. A woman's true expression is what she says at the moment. It is the current state of her feelings. It could change every five minute. I don't know how many times some of my female friends have said they would do it, only to change their mind very quickly.

In my early days of dating, I used get upset when women didn't live up to the promises they made. It took me a while before I understood that keeping one's word was a masculine trait. When I was just starting to date, I would ask a woman out and she would answer, "I will confirm." But 99.9% of the times, she never called me back. This frustrated me and made me wonder, "How is it possible she promised to call but hasn't?" I changed my view of women as I grew in understanding.

Today, I don't expect a woman keep her word. I don't allow a woman to call me to confirm my request for a date. I tell the woman to either set up a date or let me know when it is finalized. I find it less annoying to hear that a woman isn't faithful to her word. It is funny how frequently women change their minds.

When we were first dating, I planned to take her two separate venues. As we arrived at the first venue, she informed me she would not be going to the second and she had to go home after her time at the previous venue. Can you guess the outcome? She came with me to the second location, and we had a lot of fun together.

I had many women who asked me out on a date. Although they were willing to go, when the date arrived, they did not show up. I used to be angry and call and send angry texts or just block her. That didn't work. With the knowledge I have today, I try to keep my head down but let her know it was not right. I'm sure most of these women could give me a good explanation. We would then have a great time going out together.

Here's the thing: no matter what woman says or does to you, don't let her think that she can control your body. Keep it positive. Keep it positive. Be playful and don't be angry or offensive.

Don't let disappointment get you down if you can't obtain something from another person. Strength and happiness come from within. A woman should not be your motivation. You are rock and know exactly what you do with her or without. Listen to your woman but then make the best decisions from your deepest heart. You are a leader

Chapter 19: How do you identify and choose the best places?

I bet that you're asking yourself, "If not at the restaurant where can I take her?"

You're now ready to hear me out, but I must first remind you of one secret to a great date: It is not about impressing her or kissing her. It's about making her laugh and having fun. (Please note: Don't pretend to be the fool. You don't have to be funny and polite at all costs.

Try to impress her by telling her what you're not is a poor attempt at deceit. It will not lead you to lasting results. It's not unusual for women to say, "I thought that you were different", or "I expected more" from you. This is because you gave the impression that you are a superior person and you hide your true self behind flattery.

If you make women have fun and happy moments, it is likely that they will want to be with you again.

Attention, it's important to make it clear that I am not encouraging you to tell your wife jokes. I am telling you to make your partner do something you like.

You can take some time to reflect on all the activities you enjoy. I am a man and know that fantasy and imagination are not skills we can master. I have some suggestions for you:

*What courses will you be taking?

Kung-fu, guitar, yoga, dance, drawing, foreign languages...

*What other sports do you practice?

Tennis, swimming, volleyball...

*What are some of your hobbies? What do your spare hours look like?

Go on a bike ride, read, and volunteer.

Think of your most treasured places, places that you find yourself connected to, and places in the vicinity that you might be interested in.

EXAMPLES

Park, Library and your old school, Sports Center

You now have to ask these questions in order to find the perfect place for you to go on your date.

Is it accessible on foot from the meeting place or another local location on the list?

Is it a place that is frequented by many females?

Is it in a public area but private enough that you can speak privately?

Once you have answered all three questions YES, you can highlight the location that meets your needs.

Are you still undecided? Now comes the fun.

It doesn't matter if you do not have to do everything with her. Rather...

It is important for you to get to understand each other, build good memories together.

In order to keep an event fresh in our memories, it is essential that we associate it with intense emotion. To make someone feel good, it is a good idea to do several things at once and to link them to a subject.

As stated in the previous chapters, you must excite and allow them to experience all emotions. You can take them more places and plan multiple stages on a single date.

This will allow her to feel like the time they spent together has gone by quickly. A friend will ask her about it and she will have many great stories to share.

How many places must I take her every day?

Minimum 3. Better to have 5, or 7.

What is the best length of stay for each place?

Sometimes, even five minutes is enough. It all depends on how much time you have available and what you intend to do. It is okay to move. You do not have to stay there for hours. If you give them the dates, be realistic about how much time it will take and how long you will need to get there.

Do I have the obligation to explain everything from time to time? Do I have all the information to give her in advance?

It doesn't matter what she knows, all she needs is the location and the purpose. The rest of the details must be completely unexpected. You have to stop at other locations as if you didn't plan.

What should I do if she isn't interested in taking a step?

Skip it. Instead, choose another location. It doesn't matter if there are 7 or 10 places you chose, but it won't change.

Is it more fun to go to the gym or feed the animals at the parks?

A date should always include physical activity with your partner, such as a sport or a team game. You can take a stroll in the park, or you can do yoga in a park.

Chapter 20: How You Perfect The Dialogue: Topics, Tips and Tricks

You've probably ever been in an embarrassing position where you were silent in front of women. These gaps are filled with banality. The problem is that if it becomes boring, she might think you are boring.

Remember, it's up only to men to redirect conversation to more intimate and deeper topics. Don't wait to see if she responds.

If you see that the discussion is headed for a dead end you can take responsibility to restart it by changing the topic or engaging in something else.

Let's discuss the top topics to talk with women before we get into the details.

Formula One and Football

Computers and Videogames

Topics that are too logically and technically complex

Avoid ideological clashes, such as politics and religion

No negative or sad topics

The following are things you should avoid:

*Focus on a topic in an unfavorable and pessimistic manner (it happens most often to be about politics: avoid this topic).

*Complain constantly about society or people (be careful how you talk on work, transport, and weather).

*Do not talk about the past, but stay anchored to it.

*Ask her inane questions one after the next

In reality, topics are less important for women than they are for men. It is important for both of you to be able to contribute to the conversation.

The desire of a woman is to feel intense emotions. Talking to a lady does not mean giving concrete information. Communicating at 360 degrees to her is a way to communicate with her. Your words must excite and convey passion. Tell her how it was. Be expressive, move around, use a warm tone, and involve her. Let her experience the moment as if you were there.

This is not a way to succeed. Give yourself enough time to talk, take breaks, and describe smells, colors, and moods. It's easier than you think. If you're going to be telling someone about yourself, don't worry about the facts. Instead, try to recall the feelings and experience. Doing this will make it easy to get her engaged and passionate in no time.

The most interesting topics for women:

Psychological and social relationships, interpersonal relationships, differences between men, women, communication, behaviour, friendships.

Intimacy and sex;

Capacity and ability. What are you skilled at? Which are your strengths? And she?

Recent and planned vacations

Childhood (cartoons, adventures and catastrophes, classmates ...)

Dreams, Passions.

You have achieved your personal goals and you are satisfied with what you have done.

Look at fashion and clothing.

This broad topic will help you tell your stories emotionally. It doesn't matter if you're talking to a woman. All you need to do is listen to her and join in the conversation.

Respond to her earlier comments when you get the chance to show you've listened.

Attention! When we say Listening, we also mean "emotional hearing", which is understanding her mind, feeling at the moment, and in the case of a personal tale, how she felt that day. Then, you have to take off the mask of her words.

Women want an active, positive man who can see the future. They want to find happiness in the future. They will not understand the present if they remain anchored to the past, and have no interest in the future.

Now, before you begin to think about how you will meet your date, think about what you can do to feel at ease with yourself.

9 out of 10 topics have to be related to something you've experienced in recent times. Do not tell her your whole life story.

The conversation will allow you to discover if she has the qualities you desire in a woman.

You don't have to ask her questions about her musical tastes and favorite clubs. You don't always have to agree with her opinions when you reply to her. Instead, speak up and ask questions.

I will repeat that the date is to get to know each other better and become more interested in her passions. It is also about discovering who she is as a woman.

Do not try and impress her with flattery. It will only increase her interest in your company if you don't try to impress her like the other 99.9% of men.

Women value men who have the courage to stand up for their views, even when they are different from those around them.

You can have a positive conversation with her. Talk about your recent experiences, share your thoughts and feelings, discuss certain events, and even confront her on different topics. Both of you will be happy to leave the conversation with a positive impression.

How would you describe her? Be honest about what you think she is like and what it means to you.

To give an example, if she is speaking to you about her sister, you could tell her "you must really love your sister," These simple statements allow for you to get in touch with your sister and better understand her.

Let's take a look at what it is that we can do.

Avoid asking questions that have a yes/no response as much as you possibly can. A short story can be used to introduce the topic you wish to discuss.

Describe the emotion you had on that occasion.

Do not interrupt her when she talks. Instead, listen attentively and ask questions to get a better understanding.

If your opinion differs from hers calmly and calmly communicate it. If it coincides, offer her a sincere compliment based upon what she said.

Take what she said to you and make a statement about it.

Joke with her if you have the chance. It will increase the attraction between the two of you and create sexual tension.

Simply combine the conversation with the current location. These are examples you can link with the previous chapters:

*While you're there, stop by the travel section to start talking about your last trip alone and holidays.

*You pass by a Chinese place and the next time you tried to make almond chicken, it was a disaster (independent);

*You approach your elementary school to tell them that MacGyver was your favourite TV show when you were a child. After realizing it was fake, you started to watch Sailor Moon (funny).

*Meet your friends, and tell her what you're planning for the next week (sociable).

*While in a clothes store, try on accessories and ask the woman what makes you more attractive (casual). When you reach the cash desk, instead of complaining about the long queue, continue to talk to the lady, emphasizing the things (optimistic).

*She asks for information about work.

*When you are in a park, you point out some flowers/plants/insects and explain your relationship with nature (intensity and passion);

*Sit in front of a couple and talk about your views on relationships and what you're looking for in a partner (serious).

As you may have noticed in brackets, I have included what you might say to the girl speaking about that topic.

Conclusion

Dating isn't difficult. If you play your cards correctly, you will find the woman of you dreams and your happily ever thereafter. It is easy to follow these steps religiously and truly strive to be the greatest version of yourself.

Every single move counts and can help you get closer to real love or learn more about yourself. Always be honest with the woman you're going out with and never give up.

Keep in mind that you are the only one responsible for your actions. While you can improve yourself, it is impossible to change others. Go out with your head high, your chin up and your heart open. It doesn't have to work out.

This book offers practical advice and support for men who have given up hope on true love or simply wait for their soulmate to appear. Since you are reading this book, it is likely that you have already read it.

www.ingramcontent.com/pod-product-compliance
Lightning Source LLC
Chambersburg PA
CBHW050402120526
44590CB00015B/1790